Peaceful Manual

By: Rus Nikita

Copyright

Copyright © 2021 by Universal Intelligence Inc.

All rights reserved. This book or any portion thereof may not be reproduced or used in any manner whatsoever without the express written permission of the publisher except for the use of brief quotations in a book review or scholarly journal.

First Printing: 2018
ISBN: 978-1-387-92358-8
Universal Intelligence Inc.
30 N Gould St.
Sheridan, WY, 82801
http://www.Peaceful.ooo

Table of Contents

--- Preface ---
How to Read this Manual
--- Words of Caution ---
--- Intention ---
--- The Basics —

ONE: I am a Luminous Being
TWO: I am Love, Peace & Light
THREE; I Create My World
FOUR; I am Healthy, I am Wealthy, I am Peaceful
FIVE; EVERYthing is on Purpose
SIX: Love Conquers All
SEVEN:I am Honest, Caring & FREE!

Appendix: All 7 Peaceful Master Mantras

--- Preface ---

Beyond gender, race, religion, color,
predisposition, or current circumstance,
Love Unites Us All.

This manual is for *EVERYone*.

How to Read this Manual

This is a complete energy transformation program.

It will cleanse you of negative thoughts, anything that disempowers or holds you back.

It follows the universal law of creation.

It is created *with care*: *EVERY*thing written here is intentional.

Here inside this training, you will find **7 Peaceful Mantras and 7 Tools of the Peaceful Master**.

They will become part of the fundamental structure of your *Peaceful* self.

There are three things to keep in mind while reading this manual:

1. *Go Slowly, Take Your Time, Assimilate, Repeat*

This is Crucial

There needs to be sufficient time for you to think about what you read, be able to digest it and to create new neural pathways, connections, and alignment.

We will discuss this later…

Each chapter is named for a mantra and each chapter ends with a description of the mantra.

Commit the mantras to memory and assimilate them into your being.

Carry them with you going forward.

You will need at least a day to assimilate each mantra. Go Slowly.

This is very, very important; it's paramount.

The more time you take to build your foundation the stronger your resolve will be in challenging times.

Since we live on this plane of existence we are almost guaranteed to have some potentially very difficult times that we face.

You may be in the midst of some turmoil right now, just breathe, all will pass.

By creating space you can always create more freedom, that is exactly what the *Peaceful Introspective's* are for.

Here in the blank spaces, you can create more peace.

Just answer the questions, think deeply about them or better yet, write them down and capture them.

This is meant to guide you to a new perspective, understanding, and level.

If you are here…

then you are here for a reason.

Stop Looking For Excuses

Trust the Process

Peaceful Introspection

How am I feeling right now?

How to Use Mantras:

To start, repeat the mantra 11 times, and use the mantra when you feel out of alignment.

In that case, start with 11 times and keep repeating as long as necessary.

2. Trust the Process

If or when you find yourself asking: "Why and How, Does this Work?"

STOP IT. Trust the Process.

These pages are filled with ageless wisdom that has been concentrated into a highly potent, engineered life-elevation system.

It will guide you to the best results as fast as possible.

You may also find yourself thinking that this manual jumps around a lot.

If that is what you are thinking, well then of course you are correct, let it go.

EVERYthing is on Purpose - Trust the Process.

3. Read it Entirely, Finish it Completely!

Only start this manual if you are committed to completing it.

Unapplied information can become **harmful.**

Additionally, undertake this challenge **only** if you are **fully** committed with your *Mind, Body and Soul.*

Peaceful Introspection

What would my life look like if I was fearless?

--- Words of Caution ---

Sometimes assimilating the ideas from this manual will not always be easy.

Chances are this might be one of the most difficult challenges you have ever undertaken.

Control of the self is akin to enlightenment.

You will grow tremendously.

Parts of this might be very painful and uncomfortable.

Nevertheless true inner peace lives outside of your comfort zone.

By following this manual, without deviation, it is possible to attain what you seek.

By committing to this or any system you are entering into contract with the Eternal Universal Energy, *The Source*.

Deviations from your commitments is like breaking a vow between you and the universe.

This can lead to devastating, unforeseen and undesirable repercussions.

<u>You have been warned!</u>

Congratulations, you've already completed the most difficult part, the start.

Now you must simply let go and allow the universal intelligence to permeate your *Mind, Body, and Soul.*

Peaceful Introspection

What does being really peaceful look like to me?

--- remember ---

EVERYthing is on Purpose.

Integrating peaceful practices and mantras into your being will set you free.

--- Intention ---

The purpose of this manual is to train you to access your master creator power.

Although this may currently seem like an impossible task, after completing this perfectly engineered life-elevation structure you'll be able to achieve inner peace under any circumstance.

When you are able to do this you will be a *Peaceful Master.*

--- The Basics ---

This universe, and specifically the world we live in, is a very precisely engineered mechanism.

There are strict rules that govern everything around us.

Here is a perfect example:
Can you think of someone who is unhealthy, overweight, or even obese? Chances are they didn't get like that overnight.

It was most likely consistent negative health and nutrition habits that caused their current circumstances.

Conversely, the greatest athletes in the world, even if they have predisposed or natural talent, still have to put in a massive amount of energy and time to stay on top of their game.

The same goes for heroes of industry and business. They consistently create positive thoughts and actions in a focused direction, to bring to life the amazing things we benefit from.

We admire them because they are able to persevere through all the challenges, forsaking the naysayers.

You must be just as determined towards your quest for total inner peace. You must decide to be ruthless with your negative thoughts and banish them from existence.

This manual will show you how to do exactly that, even in the most challenging situations.

Nothing worthwhile was built overnight, or in one thought. It takes consistent positive actions to achieve meaningful results.

By allowing any negative or disempowering thoughts into your life, you create more negativity for yourself.

The purpose of this manual is to remove *EVERY* negative thought and feeling from your life.

A thought or a feeling combined with *The Source* is often called energy. Your focused energy has the power to create or destroy anything.

The systems and practices in here will teach you how to control and apply your energy.

Even though this may seem like an insurmountable task right now, after complete assimilation following the master manual to inner peace, you will feel like a completely new person.

Your world will be completely transformed.

People around you will see the light of peace shine from within you.

Your biggest challenges will seem to create solutions of their own, and your dreams will come into reality.

When you are able to activate your infinite power, you will be operating on the same level as universal creation.

This is what allows huge enterprises, towering skyscrapers, and magnificent spaceships, and other incredible achievements to be created seemingly without any resistance.

When you learn to operate on the level of your soul's universal power, anything and everything will be possible.

You Are Ready!

During this process you'll realign your *Mind, Body and Soul* with your *Life's Purpose*. Let's start with your brain.

Unfortunately it is inevitable that most likely you have been negatively programmed by your parents, society, and the media.

It's time to let that all go!

This manual will help you remove all of your negative auto-thoughts which occupy your habitual mind, thus creating more chaos.

Throughout this manual you'll learn seven distinct Peaceful Mantras, sometimes called prayers or incantations… commit these to your soul's memory.

Repeat them with vigor, every time you feel stressed, frustrated or upset.

Focus only on the incantation and allow every negative thought and feeling to fade away.

By doing this you will bring true light into the darkness, and even the deepest darkness cannot survive in the presence of light.

Besides the incantations, you'll also learn different exercises or practices which are engineered to elevate your mind, energy, immune system, and help you create solutions to even your biggest challenges, instantly.

Let's go over the details right now.

It all starts with breath, your breath specifically. If you are breathing, and let's assume that you are since you are reading this manual, for now just realize that: **You Are a Luminous Being!**

Peaceful Introspection

What does freedom mean to me?

STOP!!!

Every word in this manual is engineered to guide you to achieve your soul's highest potential:

Your *Life's Purpose*

It's your imperative duty to pay attention to every word here…

Peaceful Introspection

Do I still get excited about change?

ONE:

I am a Luminous Being

Everyone in existence is here for a reason, thus if you are here now, this means you have purpose no matter what others or even yourself may think.

And... Since you are here for a reason that means that you are undoubtedly an *Omnipotent Luminous Being.*

You have the power to create and destroy, you have infinite potential waiting to be tapped into, however it takes more than just silence and meditation to align your Mind, Body and Soul.

It takes mastery to create what you truly desire and less than a second to crush it.

*EVERY*thing starts with breath, it is the only thing that is a constant in your life from the second you are born until your last breath.

It is the only thing that will remain the same throughout your life. Your mind and body, all will change, but your breath will stay constant.

Paying full *conscious* attention to the quality of your breathing will bring awareness to your current state.

You become present.

By doing so you have just created freedom to shift anything you are facing. A single breath can bring you back to peace... A single minute can transform your whole life!

It is in the present moment that you will find inner peace.

Peaceful Introspection

How do I see myself?

In the now lives truth and freedom, there lives space. Most of us are taught to ignore the present, to either live in the past or the future.

That is because the majority of the world's mind-programming is very negative, and focuses on oppression versus expression.

A large percentage of the population, without realization, is programmed adversely by what the world tells us and direct influences like teachers, friends and family.

Most humans are unaware of how truly deep this negative mind-program really goes, that is part of the false reality.

It seems that most people have become used and even addicted to the status quo. So much so that when that comfort or certainty gets taken away, most of us are overcome by fear and dread.

Are you Fearful or **Fearless?**

The practices in here will teach you to break free from the shackles of disempowering incessant mind-noise.

Full self-expression of the *Mind, Body and Soul* is the *Life's Purpose* of every human being on this planet.

It is your birthright! You will learn how to create mind-space so that your inner light and peace can shine.

Right now, go deep within yourself and bring your focus and attention to your breath!

Peaceful Introspection
Are you in control of yourself?

--- *First Tool* of the Peaceful Master ---
Peaceful Breathing Practice

1. **Inhale** deeply for a count of *4 seconds*.

2. **Hold** your breath for *6 seconds*. This will allow the oxygen to saturate your lungs fully, this gets more O2 into your blood cells.

3. **Exhale** for *8 Seconds*. Starting with a short burst, as if blowing out a candle. This will purge all your CO2 and activate your diaphragm, which most people don't use.

4. Inhale, filling your lungs from the bottom to the top, instead of taking short sips. Most people use less than half of their lung capacity. *4 seconds*.

5. Hold for a moment to allow oxygen to saturate your cells and being. *6 seconds*.

6. Exhale slowly, yet fully and completely. *8 seconds*.

7. Repeat steps 4 through 6 for one minute.

The ratio should be: 2 Inhale - 3 Hold - 4 Exhale

In your mind count EVERY second of every breath.

Your focus will be on this specific sequence and count:

Inhale - One, Two, Three, Four, counting the whole time in your head.

Hold - One, Two, Three, Four, Five, Six. Keep the Count.

Exhale - One, Two, Three, Four, Five, Six, Seven, Eight. Focus on the Count.

Repeat as many times as necessary until you feel ALL the negativity fade and your inner peaceful light shine.

The *Peaceful Breathing Practice(PBP)* can add volumes to your lungs, mindfulness, and life when integrated completely.

This is specifically useful in a situation of immediate HIGH stress, physical pain, or emotional argument.

Also *PBP* is especially handy when you are in a situation that is just potentially stressful.

Let's say something has really upset you, like if you've been fired, injured, in a car accident or through anything stressful, small or big.

PBP can be beneficial in almost all circumstances.

Maybe the stressful situation isn't even directly involving you or something you can immediately work on or do anything about.

For example someone you love is sick or maybe they betrayed you or cheated on you or something much, much worse.

At this point, when you start to feel the anxiety creep in, NOW would be the best time to start the *PBP* you have just learned.

This exercise is also highly effective anytime you need to get into a state of high concentration quickly.

For example before an important meeting or a test, you can use this to clear your mind and eliminate any feelings of stress or anxiousness.

Whenever you are facing a difficult challenge and are pressed for time to center yourself, the *Peaceful Breathing Practice* is the perfect solution.

Remember that the most important word there is "practice," no one is perfect!

You will have times of high frustration and distress.

The reason we call this a practice is because by doing this daily you will build the necessary neurological connections that will come to your rescue in times of extreme situations.

When you incorporate this *PBP* into your daily life, you will be able to overcome any seemingly insurmountable challenge with relative ease.

Remember: ANYtime you feel out of alignment, bring your focus back to your breath, this will always create space.

Because we agree that you are an omnipotent and luminous being...

Whenever you feel out of alignment, the *PBP* will bring you back to center, back to peace.

One of the most important parts of the manual are the mantras. They begin with:

Peaceful Introspection

What is holding me back?

Mantra: "I am a Luminous Being"

Whenever you get out of alignment, especially when you are using the *Peaceful Breathing Practice,* hold this phrase in your mind… it will begin to align your Mind, Body and Soul.

Repeat this mantra over and over when you feel out of alignment, at least 11 times, then keep going, until you feel the light shine in yourself, until it is easier to believe in yourself, until you feel level again.

Say this whenever you are feeling down or are facing a potentially difficult or frustrating situation.

All of that will be transmitted and transformed into power, and you can use that energy for and clear decision-making and action.

The reason it transforms into power is because you have conquered yourself in that moment. By realizing that you can only control yourself, you are actively able to affect the outcome.

Now, if you're having a very challenging time, accessing your peace in this moment, chances are you are still punishing yourself for something in the past.

STOP blaming yourself, *EVERYthing is on Purpose,* Take a Deep Breath, In and Out, Repeat

Peaceful Introspection

If I could do anything, what would that be?

TWO:

I am Love, Peace & Light

The breath is your conduit to love and peace.

From your breath you'll learn how to access the omnipotent force of love, ever-flowing through your *Mind, Body and Soul*.

As you learn to recognize your different breathing patterns, you'll become more aware of your states that accompany them.

Self awareness is your friend.

When you are able to be present in your body, it will guide you towards your purpose.

Your breath will always tell you the truth, pay close attention to it.

> *How do you breathe when you are upset or stressed?*
>
> *How do you breathe when you are peaceful or happy?*
>
> *How do you breathe "normally"?*
>
> *How do you breathe 95% of the time?*

The last one will reveal more about yourself than you can imagine. It's about consistent actions which make us who we are, and it all starts with your breath.

If you want to change the quality of your life, you must change the basics.

So how do you change something so fundamental?

Peaceful Introspection

What is my biggest fear?

Very intentionally, by applying conscious thought and energy and integrating it into a consistent daily practice.

This will be one of the more challenging parts of this manual.

It will seem hard, because you are now applying conscious thought and awareness to something that has gone practically unnoticed.
Know this, if you do nothing else in this manual, and just integrate the *Peaceful Breathing Practice*, you'll see remarkable results.

What about those pesky little thoughts that come around one after the next?

The ones that erode goodness and dilute your happiness by finding flaws, even when none exist in reality?

How do you let go of the thoughts which are negative or no longer serving you?

How do you stop thinking about the last argument you had, or something differently you could have said or done?

How do you stop contemplating the past or allowing your mind to wander into the future?

Here is a Simple and Very Effective Peaceful System:

1. STOP Blaming Yourself. ---This is KEY! Let Go of the Past

Then…

2. Remember: *EVERYthing is on Purpose.*

And...

Peaceful Introspection
How do I respond to pain?

3. Now...Use the Peaceful Breathing Practice (Repeat Until Peaceful)

It will take some time for you to become fully aware of how little most people and maybe even you, stay in the present moment.

Conversely it will take some time for you to generate the necessary positive conditioning to consistently access your inner peace in the now.

In the moment, whatever is challenging you, it can all be solved.

The easiest way to reframe the current situation is to focus on what lives deep within your heart. If you are here now, that means deep within you lives pure love, peace, and light.

This is the mantra that will allow you to channel that purity and goodness and bring it forth into the present environment.

When you expose the darkness to the light, it disappears, when you expose any negativity to love it transmutes to power.

Peaceful Introspection

What can I influence right now?

--- **The Second Tool** of the *Peaceful Master* ---
Peaceful "Gone" Practice

It's all about shifting your focus. You want to direct your attention to the end of the thought, feeling, or experience.

Once it has finished, just acknowledge it, by saying to yourself ***"Gone."***

If any thought pops into your head again, once it's complete, just repeat: ***"Gone."***

Remember, you can do this with anything.

With any thought, feeling or experience you possess.

This creates separation and freedom from time, allowing your mind to take a step back and see the bigger picture.

When you do this exercise, your whole being becomes aware of the present moment, you become aware of the now.

When you add a label to it like ***"Gone"*** then the practice of letting go becomes anchored deeply within yourself.

You are able to create space within yourself and in that space your inner peace flourishes.

Your breath is life, if there's nothing else that you can let go of, focus on the end of each breath. With each exhalation just repeat "***Gone.***"

Do so until you feel the light of the universe, and inner peace flows through you again.

That's it!

Peaceful Introspection

What is my biggest dream?

The best part of this exercise is that you can practice it anywhere without anyone knowing. Even when there are other people around, and sometimes especially then.

When you incorporate the *Peaceful Gone Practice(PGP)* you leave all negativity in the past.

By realizing that whatever you were focusing on is in the past, and bringing your attention to the now, you create unlimited freedom.

All you have to do to create space is clear yourself of thoughts and feelings.

The *PGP* will teach you to do that in less than one second.

Each time you complete something, anything, there is an opportunity for awareness that will improve your clarity.

Incorporating this practice into your daily life will create more and more freedom in your life.

Inner peace comes from the gaps in the incessant noise of the mind which tends to occupy the human condition.

Remember: ANYtime you feel out of alignment, bring your focus back to your breath, this will always create space.

After you have done the *PGP*, and feel that the negativity, stress, or anything that was holding you back has now disappeared, it is time to fill the newly created vacuum with something intentional and positive.

This is where this chapter's Peaceful Mantra comes in.

Remember, repeat at least 11 times:

Peaceful Introspection

Why do I get up in the morning?

Mantra: "I am Love, Peace & Light"

Reaffirm and make it yours, use it sparingly, especially after any *Peaceful Gone Practice*.

It is important to fill, anchor and integrate the goodness and purity you have deep within you in the space that you create by the peaceful gone practice.

You must fill the hole you just dug up with something good, otherwise if you leave it open something that you may not want may crawl in there and wreak havoc once again.

However, when you are able to fill it with *Love, Peace and Light,* then you are also biologically creating new neural pathways.

You are building new roads in your brain and body.

These new roads are much better, more efficient, and at the end of the day leave you more peaceful and happy.

Just remember, you can drive on them whenever you want.

Keep practicing…

Peaceful Introspection

*What is my biggest **win** so far?*

THREE:

I Create My World

Now that you have the basic understanding of the ever-flowing energy inside of you, and how powerful it is, now is the time to start to create your own world.

This is NOT a hypothetical scenario or abstract thought.

Now you can start to effectively transform your own energy.

This will shape every interaction that you have; other people will begin to see the light shine from within you.

By controlling your breath, you can begin to control your thoughts.

That starts the transformation of the energy inside of you and the subconscious projection of your being into the world.

Before you even open your mouth, or think a thought, your energy travels through the world.

Every person can *feel* when there is something "off" about another person.

It comes much easier to those of us who are intuitive and aware.

By being able to control your own breathing you can see that you are truly a master creator. That anything you align your *Mind, Body and Soul* to, you accomplish.

You can use this in times of stress or anxiety. However it is most powerful in a state of peace and relaxation.

Pay attention to the universal feedback.

Peaceful Introspection

How does my average day feel like?

Pay attention to feedback.

When you feel open and excited, stay alert, *The Source* is talking.

Never discredit or minimize your gut feeling, your intuition.

When you are highly receptive to new ideas this can easily create a new pattern.

Now, let go of the old.

Realize that it's time to let go.

That it's only hurting you to hold onto the past.

Stay relaxed, joyful and peaceful, then repeat.

It's that simple to reprogram yourself.

This is when your conscience and subconscious energy has a direct connection to *The Source*.

You can use this conduit to reprogram yourself so that your actions align with your *Life's Purpose*.

It will take some practice and getting used to it, however it's very worth it.

Most people are usually resigned to living with their problems.

Thus they do not know how to elevate their thinking and energy to the level of creative solutions.

Simply by taking the initiative to seek out growth, and by researching these ideas, you are different.

You are a master creator that can shape your own reality.

Peaceful Introspection

What is my default in high stress situations?

You can always find a solution for any situation because you can shift your energy whenever you want.

You can always create space and peace for yourself, thus you are able to create space and peace for others.

Whenever something rattles you, when ANY negative thoughts or feelings start to creep in, immediately remove them from your mind by mentally or verbally repeating this phrase NOW:

"Erase... Erase... Erase" - Make sure you do it at least *three* times!

The *Peaceful Erase Practice* will allow you to quickly let go of disempowering thoughts, feelings or automatic programming which you are removing now.

It's a perfect tool for you, a *Peaceful Master*.

Remember: ANYtime you feel out of alignment, bring your focus back to your breath, this will always create space.

In that space chant:

Peaceful Introspection

How do I react to love and peace?

Mantra: "I Create My World"

Yes, you create your own world: with every breath, thought and feeling you create your own future.

It's time to decide what kind of world you want to live in, somebody else's or do you want to be the master of your own destiny?

Either way, you are already the master of your own destiny.

Now is the time to decide if you are ready to come into that power and take control of it.

Use this mantra whenever needed to create the next chapter of your life, even if it's the very next moment.

Peaceful Introspection

How am I influencing others around me?

--- **The Third Tool** of the *Peaceful Master* ---
Peaceful "Erase" Practice

This week do you best to use the *Peaceful Erase Practice* anytime you feel that you want to delete something you thought or said.

If one of these thoughts or feeling come up just say:

"Erase… Erase… Erase" - Make sure you do it at least *three* times!

This will immediately reset your system, you may feel a sense of relief and focus.

If you are still in the negative thought bubble, keep repeating until you have the feeling of inner peace back.

This may seem oversimplified, that is one of the reasons these practices work, they are simple, yet they work every time.

The reason they work is, because at first it may seem like a silly little practice…

However soon you will build the neurotransmitters that are focused on peace and you will find it easier and easier to let go of negativity or anything that doesn't serve you.

Peaceful Introspection

How can I add mindfulness to my routine?

FOUR:

I am Healthy, I am Wealthy, I am Peaceful

This is where you start to reshape and align your Mind, Body, and Soul with your *Life's Purpose*.

No matter how crazy things may seem to get, always remember:

"*I am Healthy, I am Wealthy, I am Peaceful.*"

That is one of the most useful and powerful incantations you can use.

It has a direct link to your subconscious mind, because it will always be accepted as undeniable truth, as fact.

No matter what your current circumstances are, this phrase is omnipotently healing.

It can guide you out of the darkness into the presence of your light.

The reason this works is because you cannot bring light into the darkness with more darkness.

You become what you think, say and do on a consistent basis.

So if you focus on negativity all you are creating is more negativity.

Conversely, if you focus on the goodness of life you will only create more light.

Your subconscious mind does not know the difference between a lie and truth, it will act on whatever information you program into it.

Make sure you only program self empowering messages and let go of the negative ones.

Peaceful Introspection

What is my biggest obstacle?

"I Am Healthy."

If you are healthy enough to breathe on your own, then you are healthy.

Even if you are in a huge amount of physical pain you are healthy.

Even if your entire body is completely deteriorating or shutting down, you are healthy.

If you are still breathing, then you can create space and there... you can achieve anything.

So if you want to be pain free, create it by incanting: "*I Am Healthy.*"

Peaceful Introspection

How do I want to change the world?

"I Am Wealthy."

This refers to your mind.

You are wealthy in so many ways.

This peaceful mantra manifests abundance.

If you are present enough to have a conscious thought, then you are wealthy.

No matter how terrible your previous programming was, now matter how emotionally or psychologically torn you are, if you can have your own singular thought, you are wealthy.

If you are smart enough to understand this manual, you are wealthy.

All you have to do is apply that wealth and create even more by incanting: *"I Am Wealthy."*

Peaceful Introspection

How do others perceive me?

"I Am Peaceful."

There is a reason this one is last.

You may not feel peaceful yet, however, this is where neurological programming comes in at its finest.

The first two incantations are undeniable truths, thus logically the third must follow suit.

This means that both your conscience and subconscious mind will accept the third incantation as truth, simply because being *Healthy & Wealthy* puts you in power of your attitude.

When you use the immutable *"I am,"* you inevitably link it all together.

The catch is: whatever you think, feel and say, you will become!

Because each present moment connects you directly to the source.

This is why this full incantation is so powerful, even if you aren't feeling joyful or calm.

This single incantation will bring you back to center and back to inner peace.

If you want to see results quickly it can be very prudent to incorporate your mantras into your daily morning and evening practice.

When you want to always have consistent results then follow the universal law of compound interest: **repeat your mantras in this precise order 11 or more times, daily, without fail, forever.**

Anytime you feel negative thoughts, emotions, anxiety or fear, use this incantation to center your *Mind, Body and Soul.*

Peaceful Introspection

What is my "worst" habit?

This incantation alone will transform your world if used consistently and often.

The more you repeat the incantations, it activates the universal law of compound interest, a powerful device of life changing proportions.

Always remember to enjoy yourself during any mantra, practice or exercise, it will help accelerate and assimilate the process.

Reciting this peaceful mantra after meditation or a mindfulness exercise will drastically speed up the integration.

Peaceful Introspection

What would I build if obstacles didn't exist?

Mantra: "I am Healthy, I am Wealthy, I am Peaceful"

Integrate these powerful incantations into your life.

Strong incantations are one of the most useful tools you have at your disposal.

Every *Peaceful Master* knows how powerful their own thoughts, feelings, language and energy are, use them wisely.

At the end of the day you are the sum of your parts. You become what you speak of, you can elevate only as high as your greatest dreams and imagination.

That is why you must start with the basics.

Prove it to yourself.

Use this transformational *Peaceful Mantra,* and the universe will unlock its secrets to you.

Peaceful Introspection

What are my most important values?

--- **The Fourth Tool** of the *Peaceful Master* ---
Peaceful "Writing" Practice

One of the most powerful tools for the peaceful master is being able to write without stopping, until everything is left on the paper.

From now on whenever you wake up in the morning, write down your thoughts for the first 10 to 15 minutes, right until there's nothing negative, stressful, or fearful left inside.

Now, when you first start doing this, it may seem and feel very overwhelming. At first, do not despair, with daily practice it will get much easier.

When you write down what you are thinking or feeling, that action has the uncanny ability to leave it all on the paper.

Typing is not the same, the visceral action of moving your pen or pencil across paper is very important, however, not a dealbreaker if you must type, then type.

If for some reason you are not able to do either, with modern technology, you can at least dedicate some time to voice dictating.

It is very important that you create a daily practice which allows you to release all of your negativity.

Learn to let go of your fears, stress, and anything that does not serve you and leave it on the paper.

Peaceful Introspection

Where is my home?

STOP!!!

NOW

Knowing what you now know…

it would be INSANE for you to take ANY part of this lightly!

Peaceful Introspection

How do I relax?

FIVE:

EVERYthing is on Purpose

There is a plan at work even if you don't see or understand it.

It's not always your job to figure out why something has happened.

If you are patient the answer will be revealed to you when you are ready and occasionally... answers are not found.

Since your future is created in the present, ask yourself:

"Is my focus and attention fully here and now?"

"Am I truly realizing the best outcome of this moment?"

"What could I be missing, that is right in front of my face?"

These Peaceful Questions are powerful and can result in profound realizations and occurrences.

Heed their guidance wholeheartedly and know whatever may have happened to you even one second ago, it has already passed.

Dwelling on the past or daydreaming about the future will only temporarily hold off whatever it is you are avoiding, often to your own detriment.

Avoiding a challenge or something uncomfortable will only exacerbate the issue.

Peaceful Introspection

How can I let go of whatever is holding me back?

Which is why it is so important to consciously identify a map of the activities you find to be the most important in life and practice daily studying and knowing it.

Avoiding what you must face, be it your pain or discomfort, will compound the difficulty.

Waiting is one of the quickest and easiest ways to create more pain, even if there was none before.

Living in the past or the future will create pain because you're not paying full attention to the now and that makes finding out what you haven't realized you've been waiting your whole life for that much more difficult to reach.

Focus and evaluate your own reactions and avoid, at all costs, being distracted by the actions of others.

How you react to challenging situations is often the indicator of your strength and character.

Overanalyzing the past, spending hours, days or weeks, thinking about something you cannot change can lead to suffering.

There is one simple reason you cannot change it, because whatever happened is in the past.

Dissecting every thought, feeling and action, can actually lead to a loss of peacefulness.

We need to be willing to release what happened in the past.

There are lessons in everything, learn them quickly and move on even quicker.

Peaceful Introspection

Why do I want peace?

If the lesson isn't revealed easily, move on, in time one of two things will happen: you will either realize the lesson or it will cease to have a hold over you.

Either way with time you'll be free, and it may take a while, however dwelling on something you cannot change will only perpetuate the internal conflict.

Let go of the past and remember that everything happens for the attainment of your soul's highest good. You have absolutely nothing to worry about, *EVERYthing is on Purpose.*

It's not until you let go of your past, only then you free yourself to create any future *you* want.

When you find yourself dwelling on the past, remember the simple practices you learned earlier in this manual.

It will take consistent practice to conquer your old patterns and reprogram non-beneficial thinking.

That is why it is imperative to take advantage of your own brain, to use your mind wisely.

When you integrate these elevating practices into your daily life you will surely be tested.

Struggles and challenges are how the universe checks commitment, only those who have integrity pass.

Those that temporarily stumble or fail, are the ones that break their word.

Usually they experience severe repercussions, and almost always lament their decision not to follow through.

Avoid breaking your word at *all* costs.

Peaceful Introspection

What brings me joy?

However when you do, never chastise yourself.

Always remember: *"EVERYthing is on Purpose."*

Then reaffirm your commitment and push through no matter what, until what you set out to do is completed.

This universe is neither for nor against you.

It is here to provide pure energetic balance, and the rewards are proportionate to the tests.

When you ask for something great, especially when it is inner peace, then the tests will be just as challenging.

Inner peace can be attained in a second, every second, as long as you stay present in the moment.

Many of us have terrible past conditioning, making us unable to appreciate the beauty of the now.

Inner peace lives in the present moment.

For those of us that want to have our peaceful self be part of our natural being, we must put effort towards staying completely present.

That means never running away from your challenges, and staying vigilantly aware of the feedback which the universe is sending you.

The first thing that we must get past is the fact that what we call *"Bad"* is usually not actually BAD.

It is your mind's projection or interpretation of the past.

There are no real bad things that happen, everything is just feedback.

Everything is cause and effect.

Peaceful Introspection

How do I nurture my relationships with others?

This relates to everything from the horrors of war to the causes of every human illness.

Humans have committed some terrible atrocities, however that is just an interpretation.

It's not "*Good*" and "*Bad*" which exist in this world. It is *Light* and *Dark*.

When we follow the light of our *Life's Purpose*, we are able to create powerfully and help others.

However those of us that choose to follow the dark are often remembered in infamy.

When used, the *Dark* energy can be just as powerful as the *Light*, the people hurt can be just as many as the people helped.

And it is in the present moment we decide which way we want to steer our energy and focus.

From the present moment we create our future.

Your choices create what happens to you tomorrow, next month, next year, and for eons to come.

Guard your current state-of-being against all evil intruders, against any *Dark* energy, especially your own!

Be very conscious and aware of your own thoughts and feelings in the present moment.

When you get tested, as all of us that strive for peace do, then remember your incantations and exercises.

Fearlessly conquer your own old destructive patterns and transform your present moment by following this manual daily.

Peaceful Introspection

How do I restore and recharge my energy?

ANYtime you feel out of alignment or are struggling to think, bring your focus back to your breath, this will always create space.

Then use this *Peaceful Mantra* to bring back to center:

Mantra: "EVERYthing is on Purpose"

If at any point you are striving to fully let go of the past, and stay present, repeating this incantation at least 11 times will help you and re-align your *Mind, Body and Soul* and find inner peace.

One of the main reasons it works is because it brings mindfulness in the now.

Yet, helps let go of the need to understand.

This *Peaceful Mantra* is very elevating and powerful. Use it often, in times of distress, fear of the future or even pain.

I know this seems contradictory.

How could the negative things that are occurring, especially if they're very challenging, uncomfortable or painful, how could they be on purpose?

Well, the truth is none of us knows the real plan.

However, it has been believed throughout the ages, and what science is coming closer and closer to proving, is that there does seem to be some kind of an intelligent design to this plane of existence.

So if we start with that, it must mean that everything is balanced, and if that is true, it means that even the seemingly negative or destructive aspects of life are actually here to guide you closer to your *Life's Purpose.*

Which means the challenges that you are facing, the seemingly huge negatives, are actually here to bring you closer to your inner peace.

Peaceful Introspection

How do I show love to myself?

I know this is a tough concept to swallow, however, it seems to be a universal truth.

However, once you do understand this, it is a very powerful shift and consciousness.

You are then no longer bound by any "negativity" that exists around you and any challenges that you face from now on will just seem like part of the process, part of your journey.

Then you will actually start to see that any potential problems are actually the reverse, they are just opportunities.

They are actually chances for you to get deeper into your inner peace.

Peaceful Introspection

What role does creativity play in my life?

--- **The Fifth Tool** of the *Peaceful Master* ---
Peaceful "Cold" Practice

One of the most useful tools of the peaceful master is to be able to find your center and inner peace during intentional cold exposure.

Recently neuroscience is catching up to what the Siberian Shamans and Tibetan Monks have known for generations: "Cold Heals."

If you really wanna elevate your peace, add a *Peaceful Cold Practice* to your repertoire.

It will do wonders for your mental fortitude as well as physical strength.

No matter what state of life you are in right now, the cold can help.

Now a word of caution, unlike the other practices in this manual, this one can cause temporary physical pain, remember this is all your mind, and the more you practice controlling yourself, the more you can conquer your mind.

Now cold exposure always works best in combination with *Peaceful Breathing Practice*, it's best to "prime your body" for at least five minutes before you dive into the cold.

Here you're going to learn a scientific technique that has been proven to lower blood pressure, increase oxygen saturation, and elevate the metabolism.

It may be uncomfortable at first, however, after consistent practice, you can truly learn to love it.

The best part about this practice is that you can add it to your morning or evening routine, however, it does work best in the mornings.

Now you can always do this without priming yourself first, and just jump right in.

Peaceful Introspection

How can I cultivate compassion for myself?

Whenever you are showering or bathing yourself, and you are ready to get out, you will start the *Peaceful Breathing Practice,* and as you do that, you will point the water directly on the back of your neck and shoulders...

Now make the water as cold as possible, yes really, go ahead and turn that knob, or press those buttons, make that water as cold as you can possibly take.

Now at first, this will be a shock to your system, your neurons are going to be screaming at you, that's OK.

This is temporary.

Go deep into your breath, let the cold wash you, feel it fully until you feel it no longer.

Make sure you stay under the cold water for at least 30 seconds, it's best to give it a minute, however, make sure you give it at least 30 seconds.

People that have done this practice consistently every day for at least two weeks have showed incredible transformations.

If you want to know more, there's now hundreds of scientific studies, proving the beneficial effects of the above practice.

Later on as you will evolve in this practice, after about a week 30 seconds will seem like nothing, that is your signal to extend it now to One Full Minute.

Continue until the minute feels like nothing that will be your signal to add another 30 seconds, or if you brave do another minute.

Very soon you're gonna go deeper and deeper into the cold, just remember to stay safe.

Peaceful Introspection

How do I honor my personal boundaries?

SIX:

Love Conquers All

Love is the single most powerful force beyond time and space.

Everything that is creation starts with love, that means that everything you see is some form of a manifestation of that ever-present, relentless, intricate, beautiful, omnipotent force.

Sometimes it may be hard to believe that even seemingly negative or very challenging things are here to bring us closer to creation, to bring us closer to love and your *Life's Purpose*.

Believe it or not, everything happens for our soul's highest and greatest good, even if at the time it temporarily cripples you.

Along the journey we all must realize that humans live finite lifespans.

May it be 3 hours, 30 days or 300 years, at some point you too will leave this physical body.

This plain is just a short stop on your soul's endless journey.

So whatever happens, even if you do not understand, it's still here to bring you closer to your *Life's Purpose*.

Put your trust in love and your life will always be filled with joy, even during times of struggle or turmoil.

To integrate conscious love into your mental toolbox, use this simple exercise:

> Whenever you find yourself straying from empowering thoughts or feelings, fill your *Mind, Body and Soul* with pure and powerful love.

Peaceful Introspection

How do I practice gratitude even in challenging times?

Focusing on and feeling the compassionate wavelengths of the universe will lead to wonderfully profound effects.

Redirecting your focus towards what you can create in the moment versus what is lacking or soul-sucking is a skill every individual must master in order to become a *Peaceful Master*.

Love is absolute creation.

If it is a person that is causing this distress, then remove yourself from their presence and focus on creating and holding the space of love and understanding.

Then repeat to yourself this power incantation: "I want that person to find love." Say their name as you repeat that phrase at least 11 times.

Keep going until your own heart is filled with true joy for them.

If a past event or situation is still upsetting you, then bring love into the present moment through conscious awareness.

Know that everything happens for your highest good.

Then follow a simple exercise of incanting: *"Love Conquers All"* until you are overcome with levity and peace.

Everyone has their own journey to travel and we must only pay attention to our own thoughts, feelings and actions.

Getting frustrated or upset with someone else's actions will only bring grief.

Just like focusing on things of the past, the fact is that you cannot change them.

Peaceful Masters learn from their mistakes without dwelling or being consumed by them.

Peaceful Introspection

How do I balance peace and ambition?

We are all human and none of us are intrinsically better than someone else.

It's the choices we make that define our humanity.

We have all made mistakes and owning them builds character, while at the same time, forgiving someone for their mistakes is akin to saintliness.

Forget the past, let go of the future, and focus on love right now.

The reason *Love Conquers All* is because of the *Universal Why*.

Even if your human body has committed or suffered atrocious acts, your Soul was sent here out of pure unadulterated, unconditional love.

The very act of your creation, even if the circumstances were horrific, is a pure expression of universal love.

There is a deeper framework here, many opposite energies aligned to create the very unique person reading this manual.

It's not your job to understand the *Universal Why,* you are alive now, at this time, on this level, so enjoy it.

However, it is your duty to know your *Life's Purpose*, your *Earth Why*.

This is revealed by aligning your *Mind, Body and Soul.*

That is why it is imperative that you follow the concepts expressed in this manual exactly, without deviation.

If you have strayed, do not despair, just refocus.

Go back to the principles taught here, recommit yourself, no one is perfect, we are all flawed humans doing our best to get it right.

Peaceful Introspection

What seemed impossible that I conquered?

Your true *Earth Why* may not be revealed for years, or maybe you'll get it instantly in a moment of a *Peaceful Breathing Practice*.

It's not always known when your answers will be revealed.

You will never know if you do not seek the truth.

Never worry about the timeframe...

If you are breathing, and reading this manual, know that you are a child of light, you are here for a reason. And until you discover your *Earth Why*, remember this*:*

Peaceful Introspection

What are my limitations?

Mantra: "Love Conquers All"

If you have high aspirations, chances are that challenges you'll have to overcome will be just as great.

Nothing great was built overnight.

Often all we see is the single moment of success.

Rarely do we see the years of struggle, training, failures that come before that.

Most frequently those that succeed in achieving their plans have to overcome seemingly insurmountable risks, disadvantages, and challenges.

We do not see what others had to conquer to get to their success.

Knowing that *Love Conquers All* acknowledges that "all" or *anything* can be conquered, and because we are *Love, Peace, and Light,* we can conquer anything.

If you are stressed or in pain now…

Remember: ANYtime you feel out of alignment, bring your focus back to your breath, and use this mantra when it's right.

This will always create space.

Peaceful Introspection

How can I accept things I cannot change?

--- **The Sixth Tool** of the *Peaceful Master* ---
Peaceful "Connect" Practice

Sometimes the easiest way to reconnect and reset is to connect deeply with nature.

It is a myth that you need to be in the wilderness in order to do this.

All you need is a little piece or plot of nature.

A rock or some bark can work wonders.

However, if you can go outside and stick your feet in the soil, put them directly on the ground, on the sand, on the snow.

This is the portion where you pretend you are a tree, the easiest way to do this is to hug a tree, however, if you don't want to "look weird" putting your hands up or feet on the ground will do the trick.

The key to the practice is to stay grounded until you feel the energy of the world, and a deep sense of peace will begin to emanate from inside of you.

The first couple times may be a little bit awkward, however, stay in it, it is <u>all</u> part of the process.

You can use this as a pattern interrupt anytime you feel out of shape or any negativity, creeping in.
Go
Connecting with the electrical and grounding energy of mother earth will always reset you, if you allow it.

Your job here is not to fight it, just let it go.

Peaceful Introspection

How can I create a peaceful environment?

SEVEN:

I am Honest, Caring & FREE!

During each second, minute, hour, day and week, forever be truthful with yourself.

In fact, be brutally honest! For the only way we can grow is to know where we start.

The beginning of any permanent transformation begins with authenticity.

When you truly care about yourself as a human being then you'll always be honest with yourself.

Selfcare goes beyond basic energetic knowledge, it taps into the omnipotent force of love.

It is there that you will find healing and deep inner peace.

You will be connected to *The Source* and once again feel the light shine through you.

Freedom is priceless and it's ever available for those who want it.

To be truly free all you have to do is be completely present in the moment.

In the now, the past fades and at the same time, your future becomes aligned with your *Life's Purpose*.

Being present in the now may have been a difficult thing for you to achieve before reading and assimilating this life transformational manual.

Peaceful Introspection

What does it mean to live authentically?

By daily using the simple peaceful practices described in here, you'll tap into the universal compounding force and will be able to get the results you have always dreamed of.

--- **The Seventh Tool** of a *Peaceful Master* ---
Introspective Evaluation Practice

This is something you can practice at any hour, day or week, whenever, wherever, as needed.

You will learn to dive deep into your *Mind, Body and Soul* to fully free yourself from the past and future to completely experience your inner peace at the fullest level.

Know that when you feel or focus on something fully it cannot be held onto permanently.

When something does not go your way or can potentially upset you, then instead of getting mad or irritated, ask yourself a simple question to bring yourself back to present:

"What do you think the cause of the situation is?"

Once you have a satisfying answer, ask yourself:
"Why am I focusing on this right now?"

Once you have an intimately true answer, ask yourself:
"What are the possible factors that are making me think or feel this way?"

Once you have a full answer, ask yourself:
"Is this what I really, truly want?"

Once you have that answered thoroughly, ask yourself:
"Am I at peace now?"

Once you have a good answer, ask yourself:
"What could help me balance and center?"

Once you have a proper answer, ask yourself:
"How did my past thoughts, feelings and actions cause this?"

Once you have a clear answer. ask yourself:
"Can I do anything about this right now?"

Once you have strong answer, ask yourself:
"What do I want to focus on to create a different present and future?"

Keep asking yourself questions until there are no more questions left.

Keep diving deep until you reach the bottom, and then dig a little deeper.

In order for the *Introspective Evaluation Practice* to be fully effective you must exhaust the list of your questions, otherwise some will linger in the back of your consciousness and will come back to haunt you at a later time.

At some point asking the questions may become extremely painful emotionally, psychologically or physically.

Keep going through the pain...

You are stronger than you know and there is light on the other side!

If you get stuck, return to the Peaceful Breathing Exercise.

Notice what comes up for you. In the breath, feelings and memories may come to the surface.

You may notice that things are connected in your subconscious in ways you didn't expect.

Notice them and acknowledge them without judgment.

Breathe through your revelations.

Uncover the deepest darkest parts of yourself, feel everything fully, never run away from your own thoughts.

When you come to terms with your own self, with your own thoughts and feelings, you will achieve inner peace.

Free from time, free from burdens, free to create and to be whatever you want.

Let go and you'll feel your inner peace again.

Mantra: "I am Honest, Caring & FREE!"

Repeat this at least 11 times until your *Mind, Body and Soul* are centered and you are peaceful.

Always Remember: ANYtime you feel out of alignment, bring your focus back to your breath, this will always create space.

---Postscript---

This will become a lifetime practice.

The purpose of this manual is to free you from your negative mind noise for at least seven consecutive days.

If you find yourself consciously entertaining ANY disempowering thoughts or feelings that means you have broken continuity and must start your count all over.

After enough practice you will be able to go an entire week without anything disturbing your inner peace, no matter what circumstances occur in your outer world.

In order for this manual to work the way it was engineered, you must follow all the rules exactly.

There are universal principles at play here: *Powerful Positivity* and *Uncompromising Consistency*.

When they are put together they create the third and most powerful force of this equation: *Universal Connection*.

These are the forces that shape the world you see before you.

They have created everything you see and feel, and will continue to do so long after your breath has left your lungs.

When combined they can move mountains, because they connect you directly to the source.

These principles are deeply embedded in this manual.

We are revealing them to you now, because you are now a *Powerful* **Peaceful** *Master.*

You must only use these principles to create Peace, Love and Light in this world.

Deviation from consistent positive practice causes massive, unforeseen and many times negative changes in the internal and external worlds.

You are here to let your light shine and create something uniquely beautiful.

When you align your *Mind, Body and Soul* with your *Life's Purpose* you have direct access to the Universal Source.

You are now ready to completely reprogram every cell in your body.

You now have the tools to instantly shift your energy, to always stay in alignment, and laser focus on your *Life's Purpose*.

The only thing that will hold you back is yourself.

Diverging from the program will only lengthen the time that you are without true inner peace.

The closer you adhere to these principles, the faster your progress will be.

This is a very specifically engineered system, trust the process.

Always remember every obstacle, or challenge you face no matter how extreme is just a test.

The only way you fail is to give up, to stop the internal work which brings you closer to your truth.

The only way you can achieve inner peace is to conquer yourself, to climb every mountain, explore every crevasse.

If you have made it this far, you have the power inside you, it's up to you to use it. Good luck, and always remember *EVERYthing is on Purpose!*

--- *The Eight Tool* of the *Peaceful Master* ---
Peaceful "Night" Practice

I am giving away this bonus tool, for anyone that has challenges resting, or sleeping.

In today's hectic world it seems that more and more people are having issues getting the deep relaxation that their Minds, Bodies and Soul's need.

One of the most important components to living a fulfilled and healthy life is making sure that you have enough real rest and recovery.

This can hold me happen when you are truly at peace,

Nowadays, more people suffer from nightmares, insomnia or other night related illnesses than ever before.

One of the main reasons for this is that people do not have a nightly practice to let go of that day's irritation and anxiety.

So they follow them into bed, into the dreamland, into the ethereal plane and they wreak havoc.

There is a simple solution, *Peaceful Night Practice*, which you can easily create for yourself.

You can use the same journal you use in the morning, or if you would like to keep a separate one that is completely fine, what matters here is the consistency of this practice.

Every night before you are ready to settle in allow yourself 10 to 15 minutes to write down answers to these questions:

   1. *What is still bothering me from today that I'm letting go of right now?*

2. How could I have been or reacted better today?

3. What is at least one positive or beautiful take away?

Allowing the action of writing down and releasing any negativity you will strengthen the new electrical connections you are building.

By looking introspectively and acknowledging where you fell short or how you could have performed or been better, you are creating new ways of being.

This will allow you to connect to something much deeper.

Lastly, by ending and focusing on something positive and beautiful, you are allowing light and peace to come into your being right before your nightly rest, this will elevate your dream and relaxation.

Appendix: All 7 Peaceful Master Mantras

I am an Omnipotent Luminous Being

I am Love, Peace & Light

I Create my World

I am Healthy, Wealthy, Peaceful!

EVERYthing is on Purpose

Love Conquers ALL

I am Honest, Caring & FREE!

Wisdom comes from practicing simple truths. It's time to stop judging and start healing.
The choice is *now* yours.

Thank you very much for purchasing and consuming this manual.

If you want to connect more and join the Peaceful Tribe visit
http://www.Peaceful.ooo

There you will find a lot more tools, techniques, and immediately applicable strategies.

If you really want to dive deep…

We have tons more stuff you can participate in:

From transformational live events, to solo journeys and guided integrations you can practice on your own.

You deserve to be *Healthy, Wealthy and Peaceful* now take the next step:

http://www.Peaceful.ooo

www.ingramcontent.com/pod-product-compliance
Lightning Source LLC
Chambersburg PA
CBHW070833300426
44111CB00014B/2537